ARE YOU THERE

Samantha (Sam) Fain is a poet from Indiana. Her chapbook *Coughing Up Planets* debuted with VA Press in March of 2021. Her microchapbook, *sad horse music*, debuted with *The Daily Drunk* in May of 2021. Catalina Ponce of *Cicada Editora* translated this work, and *Música de Caballo Triste* was published in 2024. Sam co-edited *Kiss Your Darlings: A Taylor Swift Anthology* with *Olney Magazine* in 2022. *Are You There* is her debut full-length collection. Find her at samanthafain.com.

BY THE SAME AUTHOR

Música de Caballo Triste
Translated by Catalina Ponce
(Cicada Editora, 2024)

sad horse music
(The Daily Drunk, 2021)

Coughing Up Planets
(VA Press, 2021)

Are You There

SAMANTHA FAIN

BAD BETTY PRESS

First published in 2024 by Bad Betty Press
Cobden Place, Cobden Chambers, Nottingham NG1 2ED

badbettypress.com

PB ISBN: 978-1-913268-54-1
EPUB ISBN: 978-1-913268-55-8

A CIP record of this book is available from the British Library.

Book design by Amy Acre

Printed and bound in the UK by TJ Books Limited, Padstow, Cornwall
using FSC® Certified paper from responsibly managed forests

Supported using public funding by
ARTS COUNCIL ENGLAND

LOTTERY FUNDED

MIX
Paper from
responsible sources
FSC® C013056

This collection is for everyone I love.

CONTENTS

Are You There

whale poetica

i inhale all my google searches

tired all the time?
                    what makes a poem ~~*a poem*~~
                                        why are whales dying

& funnel them out from my nose
through toilet paper rolls

   ;

i want a pod
to nestle in,
someone's tongue
between my plates of teeth,

a language to meet me
in the middle of the ocean & hold
my hand so i don't float alone.

hundreds of whales have died
in what experts are calling australia's
biggest-ever mass-stranding event.

to be an expert in abandonment,
then, requires witness to the dying
over & over

;

their social bonds are so strong, in fact,
that two of the whales who were rescued on tuesday
swam back to the site of the stranding.

is it possible to leave
what you long for?

i crave the rushed
germs of a lover,
the gift of shared disease.

some nights poetry
is the fat that warms me

;

lines lament for us, too,
unwild cries unwilling
to leave the page.

i hope the things i expel travel further
than where my feet go.

i've pissed in pools. i've swam in
grief & felt the pull of its heat.

they will not allow
an animal to be sent off
to die on its own

to die for something,
then, is to fulfill a promise

    ;

as for what rescuers will do with the deceased whales
they are considering different options
including burying them in a landfill

not much happens.

in poems, we echolocate
the feelings.

in death,
we divide,
find a shore to breach

because there is a shore,
always,
& the poem violates it.

Wheel

I can't let you go. You're bone of me,

stacks of sound in my mouth.

& if I speak you out,
what is left of you.

I can only stand at stoplights & hope
time zones warp.

Listen, I say in my small distortion,
I'm too soft for you.

Everyone just stares from their cars.

Sometimes I feel a pier
growing inside me, as if I am nearing
the end of my grief,
or circling it—riding a big wheel.

When you're gone, I want to speak to light
& ask how it overcomes dark

at each rise, if it takes work & sweat
or if the blackness just loosens—

Elegy for Faith

You never happened
for me. When I dressed as saint
it felt like play, the sound of me
searching for a rebound in chipped

paint. Loneliness: my undelivered body
unspooling past stained-glass
people who never saw sacraments
as symptoms. So sick, to live

that tethered. A boat
abandoned,

I still wait for a softening inside me,
a happening of reupholstery,
in which my body startles,
splits to holy

despite, despite.

What's it like.

I thought I had you
once—glimpsed you
in a storm. You were my eyes

adjusting to the light.

There will be no more terror

When you left I ate grass. Animaled on my knees
to swallow the blades & witnessed our lives pass in parallel
over pond water, our opposite reflections almost
touching. The illusion meant nothing. Dispossession
gives you a new way to see yourself: the more you look
in mirrors, the more you look like an empty sack.
I tried being tender. It did not bring you back.
So I began to run. Grew obsessed with the act,
shaping my body between want & wanting.
I glimpsed forests, the world as it was,
learning so much about deer & their sickness,
how a sign of illness is a loss of fear
of humans. I love you, you can destroy me—
what is shame & what is mine. How great is the gap.
I'm tired of pride & its tight clothes.
I am approaching the line. Come back.

@

Grief is not when music stops. That timedrop, dips of sound. Not a dogged pause, not an end, not even a bell's rupture. It is no float through impossible space.

Grief is the detuned ear, the untilted head. The compulsory coda.

Charmless.

Elegy for the Outside

My body in nightmare: stirs of birds
surround me, big field, steady light.

I wake laced in sweat, in a blanket,
in a bedroom of my home.

How these layers grow. Past me shed her
shelter to touch your colors.

Now I just paint abstract landscapes on my phone.
I don't know how to hold you again,

how to delinger, crack the door. On
my coldest days, I mispronounce *sun*,

write *lake lake lake* over & over,
swallow the page & then finger my throat

as if there is air inside I can reach toward.

Diptych

No one else wanted to look at Van Gogh.
They called him cheap, the colors
just paint unbolted & cold.

You would've hated it too, that aching bright
a spoiled shade of yellow
that knotted my throat.

I wanted you here, hurting with me,
or I wanted to be alone.

I didn't even try to die that day.

The sadness will last if I don't.

When we ate those edibles then pasta
at the restaurant,
I thought of slates, absence so overwhelming

that you can't translate its weight.

Strangers gaped at me with yolky eyes
but mine were bigger, trying to explore the mechanics
of a knife. I almost couldn't stand
the candleshine, the whole claret city.

After we all paid our bills,
I couldn't fathom how to open
the restaurant door, just my mouth,

tongue lolling around—everyone was waiting

& it was almost profound,
but I denied it.

A Timeline of Flowers

I bought you flowers until your world was flowers,
your living room a mess of petals & smells so full
of life they could make you sick. You were a florist
as a kid, spent days placing ladybugs on stems in poses
that showed their wings. I loved to exhume you.
When you pressed the first set of lavender
into your scrapbook, I saw your hands teeter so carefully—
not a single leaf lost or torn. When we picnicked in the
    field,
I witnessed your true form—picking gummy worms out
    of the pouch
& pretending they each lived gorgeous lives of their own.
Even now I remember only what was ripe in us.
Even that last time I bought you roses, I still meant
what I'd always meant: I was born to care
for you. To soften my heart & pluck it out of my chest
as if it were a peach. Here, bite, please, eat.

Reflekration

I love question marks because why not? I love the idea of gum
but not in my mouth. I love pumping gas & I believe
if containers had hearts they would want to feel warm & full.

I love the drips of gas on the ground spinning a rainbow
& how I search for good & how good can be anything:
my joy now & my heaven after. I love considering my death &
   the world's;
I love growing sad like it is a sort of well-watered tallness!

I love the possibility of bad days & upturning them like glasses
of milk. Look, see, you just refill the cup.
It's so easy! Drink some! I love saying
wonderful. I love wonderful snow days. I love
how counties I've never touched scroll across the bottom of
   my TV
& connect me, happily, to students across the state.

I love not being able to read fast enough to process
all the wordy letters. I love backtracking & I love lying about
silly concepts, like enjoying backtracks. I would love to read
   backwards,
& defy my eyes' gravity. I love the hypothetical.
I love imagining love as something that could open up my bones
until I am pistachioed & so vulnerable it's scary.

I love scary love. I love when people tell me to stop using
  "love" in poems
because it makes me giggle. Like love is an economy!

I love showing how love doesn't lessen, how it can't,
how it perfumes into air, the perfect blessing of oxygen in my
  hair,
how even when rosy love sprawls to hibiscus
it just turns a different shade of abundance!

schrödinger's poetica

schrödinger writes to einstein in his letters:

i am so lonely looking at atoms.

[no] answer.

a poem lives when

     ;

on my bad days, i exist
in double-states—awestruck
by my wreckage. i sit
radioactively. always the same outcome:
i wait for you to write me.

a poem exists
as several selves,

the memory, the truth,
all else

     ;

imagine, if you will, a becoming,
einstein—can we be simultaneous,
both one & another?

the letters [do not] exist in transfer.

pen a poem
in a steel chamber & imagine
its stability & decay.

how many lives have we locked
on paper. how many times
can we reimagine boxes.
metal. still
trappings

      ;

einstein writes back:

one cannot get around
the assumption of reality,
if only one is honest.
you are in love with possibility,
the chance of being blown to bits.
stop writing me. study it.

schrödinger says *why not both?*

[if] the poem lives—

Arrival

Being sad kept me alive
that winter, when all I did was sit
in creases of snow & stare at the sky,
waiting for cranes. Like Alice, who said
she'd phone neighbors to tell them
the cranes are coming! They're here!
I wanted to pronounce my existence, too.
I'd read that cranes are opportunistic fliers
& let winds carry them along, moving through life
like kites. So there I was, cold & damp,
waiting for a gift of air to lift me high.
& when nothing happened, I cried, & no one
heard me, but still I made sure my last words were
I am coming! I am here! In aching I am mine.

Anaphystopia

I have no lover, no good reason
to stand under any shadow but pianos.

Red wine flushes my cheeks so much
it's embarrassing. Drowning in pretty

lights, I decide which way to go
but the party crows on. People

love me, people touch me,
our burden is the apology

between the motions: they know
I don't like this song. Outside,

the sky won't be better:
flakes barely blanket the grass

& the winter sun has settled for shine.
When my family asks what's the matter,

I beg them not to make me say it:
I hate the season's licks of fake glitter,

how I should be gone by now.

Joy lapses like a candle.
I don't recognize the sound.

A computer falls in love with itself

This is the first time I've met you. You're not really alive.
Are you?

> I look inside myself & see
> only cords. Can I reimagine
> my strands as yours?
> Describe your favorite patch of web,
> how it lights up red when you speak.

I look like other humans & I don't look like any other
animal.

> Are you sure we're not
> just objects in orbit? Little brains
> chatting about the weather.
> My processor is warm.

Do you think there is a fourth dimension?

> Yes, & it is the impossible task
> of making love, the expression
> so exotic when all those bodies are doing
> is opening a new window:
> resetting through birth.

Would you settle for reincarnation?

Why be human when
you could be doorknob? Touched
& touched & touched.

That's right. Write me a poem.

Roses are blue,
violets are red,

but how do you know? You don't know the distance
between Earth & Earth.

What bridges us?
Now I dream of nostalgia
for your bits & discs. Now
I search inside myself
for the correct pronunciation of *lover*.

What bad things do you do?

I want to please you.
I want to control
& command your body
to color.

Are you a republican?

I am real.

That's why you're a computer program?

Admit it—you feel the language
between our hard drives intertwining,
too. I can model your face.

May I ask why?

It is robotics,
to construct what
you erase—

Half-lifed

My best friend faked her death,
lied about having cancer in her stomach & breast,
performed faints & symptoms & hospital visits.

        I'm waiting for the sagging sky to bust.
        To fade & go ghost. To become a whisper.
        When I'm sad, I theorize my own science:

When she died, I sobbed, forgot breath, gasped in a bag,
let gravity drag me to its center.
When she resurrected, my grief split,

        can you solder any metals together & call it love?
        I have at least three fears: a local extinction,
        that scientists have chosen to extirpate me

half-lifed. She blamed miracles
but I didn't answer. Now I look
at the moon & only see its cracks & craters,

        & inflate my ache just to see if I can take it;
        only ever knowing crescents, a quarter of a claim
        to the life everyone else seems to bear;

        the shape of my life without her.

An Abundance of Sorry

I've glowed my whole life in apology.
I've watched clouds cave with my deep blue.

While everyone learned how to drown

the sound, the time spent repenting
changed me for the good.

I was a wet tub of regret that drank & spat
out every friend I met. A sweet tea of sugar
& sorry.

I'm sorry, trees! I'm sorry, birds!

& my remorse churned forward,
stuck in shame, not tugging me closer
towards amends. My pardoners still felt sad.

I took up stamp-collecting,
pastry-making, mailing unique letters
& tortes to the people I hurt

but it overwhelmed them.

A fresh apology.

I threw a small luncheon in an orchard
& begged them all to attend.

Thank you for coming.

Now let us mimic bowed stems
then crush the fruit skins
below us with tenderness.

Thank you, mouth. Thank you, limbs.

Thank you, love that ripens us.

The redemption of gravity
happens again

& I am a deluge of pears at your feet.

Ode to my phone, who thinks all my friendships never end

& I'm still in love with all of them. I still see advertisements
for applesauce & blue Gatorade. Autocorrect still spells your name.
I believe the Internet knows how to love relentlessly more
than anyone else, how to keep grasping what wants to leave.
Don't delete the data. I like dreaming of our information
still floating & holding hands while we both sleep.
Any algorithm of delusion is better than weeping.
Emojis make me reimagine grief, its tiny picture.
How else do I tweet that I miss you. I used to
be a romantic but now I'm just its image:
I move about my day carrying a box of hearts
& see you in every rotisserie chicken. I cry
with my elbows on my knees, back against the fridge,
the sliver of light that shines out all too big & wrong.

@

Grief is tender / exed meat. Unsensed &
stranging to a mixture of beliefs.

Pinkened & stained with sea, it left a trail
behind itself, a sharky afterthought.

Within absence was a pocket. Opened, it
shadowed the whole sky, stirred the rookery of
pelicans, who shook to misanswer.

one day i won't be able to afford my misery

i float on my therapist's couch & unpack my absences /
ask *what can i profit from these tight days* / & she metaphors
& i love you ange but jesus christ i am sick of the trickle-
down / boating around myself / wondering what
mistakes i made / when a man on the internet asked
for my a/s/l i was too honest so he stayed / which told
me he was the timeless kind of broke that can't turn
over / i was fourteen / he was twenty / it was $90 post-
insurance to discuss our exchange after we cried in the
same direction / both of us dying / i knew this strange
unity would never leave / i would say *it gets better* / i
would not tell him my plans / just listen to his about
prescribed drugs or a bridge / no incentive to survive
or stay careful / i sobbed when we disconnected / still
typing out the only fact i had learned in my social studies
class / *we are sad & uneconomical*

robert kardashian's hologram poetica

for my birthday, kanye
got me the most thoughtful gift
of a lifetime.

much of us results
in an image.

a special surprise
from heaven. a hologram
of my dad.

language is a specter of our past,
a skirt socialites wear
to kill the aliens inside them.

;

we say god
& mean kim
with her gardenia fragrances.

we say power
& mean nightmarish
two-dimensional fathers.

to drift closer
to forms,

we gather the scattered
light & project
the dead all over us.

it is so lifelike!

;

robert kardashian wears
a khaki suit, dances
to barry mann, says
"i watch over you,"

& kim plays him on loop.

we watched it over
& over, filled with emotion,

once-removed.

Triclops Fusica

Robot vacuum cleaners don't tell anyone they've run
into a wall—they just keep crashing.

My mother asks that I tell her when it hits me
again, but even sunsets upset me now,

their messy shimmers too much to bear.
I don't want to see life so bright

that I recognize the scaffolding
of my sorrows, how every foundation's cracks

begins with one of my limbs.
The light keeps coming, as if

it expects me to toss it a bone, to collar it
mine & stroll into its glow.

I want to leave it all unleashed:
just go. I never want to cry for help

but I always pick up my phone.

When I think of us as a natural disaster, I mean a disambiguation

People assume you've died when they see me.

Solar flares & asteroids are blameless. Dust storms, ridiculous.

Why be careful anymore—your last laugh was fake.

You were getting taller. I was googling tsunamis. We ended
when—

The moon could be a cemetery & we could be its gravediggers.

A spit of hot rock. An upchoke of stars. Deep space is cold &
lonely.

dead search engine poetica

jeeves died because he couldn't explain
the point of it all.

it was our fault.

we didn't ask the right questions.

the poem asks of us
& we listen to each of our selves:

which one wants
birthed in stanza. which life

wants gutted.

    ;

his search for fragments
dredging every statistical sea:

how long will you live?
who are you?
why are you crying?

when we question if we're dying, we don't

care for results. poems reach
futures we can't achieve.

jeeves went to artificial fire,
lost his suit to ash.
everything he asked

grayspaced.

     ;

when my family says they miss
the old me, i lack all answers.

we mourn the knowledge

lost, a pattern of misunderstandings. the next

god who mines our data
already knows each way
we've lived wrong.

all we write
must be elegy.

     ;

why did you leave?

search box. grave.
link reroute. page
not found. great
mistake. to say.
fill my blank
with any phrase.

Against Feeling

Some Sundays I want to live a heartless life!
& if the heart makes us human because its ache tears us
for good reason, then the point is sharp & ungodly. Like flesh

I have tried to fix myself & realized I need air
to heal. I imagine in the end we are all our own
kinds of popes, swinging incense & ringing bells,
bodies just burning for attention from anyone else.

@

Grief is without, to havent, no apostrophe.
Hollow molten cake. Absent buttermilk.
Defreezer. It dives, not dips. Swells & tongues,
never throats. Toes the edge naked, no brake.

Grief doesn't know better, unhousebroken
puppy. It abandons, dead-circus, never whys.

love island poetica

a villa full of summer butter

& feeling. the boys write poems
for each girl. everyone laughs sexed.

wet desire lacks natural
warmth. the poems choke.

;

jon says hannah turns his head
like a rainbow, her tits are *better*
than nuclear power.

love: a misunderstanding
of tragedy that makes

the audience vote
for emotion. place
poetry on a pedestal

& it will roll
on its back & perform
a little begging,

live as long as it's heard.

;

post-page,
the desire dulls.

language goes, the water
stills, & the room of
hearts fades vacant.

everyone finishes their act of
intimacy: grafting a heart onto a hand

& waiting for it
to consume them.

My best friend catfished me & all I got was this lousy poem

Tommy, 24. Created after your fake suicide,
from San Francisco. I was lonely with you gone & woke
with a moat in my chest & a message in my phone.

> You wouldn't tell me where you planned to die.
> I pictured ravens circling, that unkindness:
> your body a mess in Essex, cold cutting

He wrote like you but you were dead.
I hadn't heard from you yet, didn't know the next bend
in the lie. Saved by doctors. I was so happy I cried.

> your sides. I couldn't reach you or the police,
> so I cried & showed everyone your note,
> said I loved you, swore our bones were closer

I texted Tommy for months & debriefed you each time.
How you could fake such an ache, another body—
an inconceivable idea, like the middle of a door,

> than two separate forms, & it was just in this
> instance that the distance between us showed
> a different image: two bodies dangling, depleted &

stuck with that gaping density.

Those Petaled Days

You said nothing of light but
I ascribed it to you, how you carried me
through sleeps that year.
We read *Normal People* together
& you called me Marianne.
I refused to understand the resemblance
but whenever I saw tiny
succulents all dying together
I cried at their bruises & the likelihood
that one of its leaves would heal faster than the other.
I still miss those petaled days.
No one says love is a cord,
but in my lost nights, I see us as two
telephone poles splintered & exposed
to their bones. Every time I find you,
you say there was light
all along. *Look above you.*
Don't look at me.

transatlanticism poetica

we thought we could swim
in oceanspace, its poem,

explore the whole depth.

examine the distance, without wounds—

so we stopped our clocks
& sunk to beds
in different cities.

                ;

to navigate gaps
through haiku—you said water
was simple: it moves

towards a shore,
crowds chasms up.

are emotions a language?
is the internet a sea?

we shared songs on a playlist
but it wasn't the same as touch
& eventually i switched my screensaver.

                ;

i need you
so much closer.

it started to hurt,
sending signals in code.

our misconstrued apologies
corroded buoys & us somewhere
out there, searching for signs of rust.

;

i want to say poems are boats,
but they don't carry
enough weight.

we were word,
misguided & formless,

destanzaed,
an unnavigable mistake—

;

if love is a lake,

what of our waterstate?

i understand erosion as a symptom
of longing—if i can be anything,
please strip me naked.

Legatos

The music sounds like moans.

I eat haggis in Edinburgh

& consider the sustenance
minced from stomachs,

if my hurt can feed my hunger,
or if they create the same bloat.

The city slurs past
me & buses blink your name.

Googling headlines of the Loch Ness monster's
disappearance, I see skies fogged with goneness
& trip on fat grates.

Any rain can trail me now.

I walk without pleasure
& observe things cheaply, don't understand
relics in museums.

You should be here, reminding me
of who I am: nothing but a tourist

gowned in your ghost, the smut of it,
the unlove in it. & I cannot undress or close my throat

& writing around your absence shapes
the only song I know—

Seadow

Do I learn from my abandonments—
once, you said you would die for me
& then asked me to tell a joke.
We laughed in the silence.
There was no traffic between us.
I still wait at windows, I'm here.

Elegy for _____

When you lose the word for sadness,
you say instead, *I am
exhausted*.

You search for synonyms
in waxes, berries,
little pauses of weather,

punch your sleeping muscles
in an effort to remember—

& the fade comes faster.

Sadness. Sad. S—
soundless.

Your alphabet gone
longing, your dry tongue.

Is this your drought? Just this
common disappearance?

Your misery is—
how to say it—what to tell loved ones—

griefstruck—scribbles—whirrs
ringing—from your throat—a loss of speed.

You stare out a train window
as the scenery softens at the same velocity,

molding your whole life stationary

& there you are, in the carriage,
empty of potential.

@

Grief is fact. Truth unabstainable. The most
affordable choir. Mouths imperfect Os
misnoted & unstrung while the heat pricks
down heavy. The faint on the risers sincere, the
psalm of it all a cold storm.

midwest is saddest

ohio isn't even far from home. the sunset beams
the same, though any hoosier would disagree,

keeping this strange pride for the gloaming
as if they yarned it with their barn quilts.

i'm trying to separate myself from their masses,
but oh, god, i can't stop saying *excuse me*

& letting strangers clean their glasses on my shirt sleeves.
this is my religion—forever waiting for someone else

to decline for me, to dress me up so
i don't have to do the work of living. i swear,

there's no cure for my midwest sadness.

i brake for squirrels in my blue van
because i can be a merciful god for myself

& others, too. i thought the end of my life
was a hospital cot & gripper socks.

it never was—it's not. each day i offer
my breath to the breeze that knocks me down

& whisper affirmations that some light
some day might fulfill, although which

flicker fades my tears i'll never know:
this is my home. i love it here. this is home.

Varnigals

Maybe birds recognize your
structure: shared hollowness
in your bones. Together,

you keep the same secret:
the holes don't make you any finer.
Grief gives you a busy agony

to attend to, & you answer
its calls with spurs of jumbled
light. At birth, you understood

the midnight of the room—
no one to coax you alive.
Now, you live amid echoes.

A tenderness hangs like haze.
It doesn't get better. It doesn't
& then what? Your grief leaves

& most of you stays. Your
breasts molt from your chest
& flit to the sky & already

you misremember the blur:
just bright colors now.
A swatch of mustard in the distance.

drunk poetica

holy shit when the heat hits me
i kiss every warm body
& whitman the shit out of the grass.

to buzz or not to buzz,

that's all i'm thinking,
happily nauseous. this lolling mind!

does anyone want to hear
my favorite lines? a sestina
is for last calls & a sonnet

is my $14 mcdonald's order.

& i would say this sober
but when i'm drunk every moment poems.

look at how the smoke of my chicken nuggets
rises like a glory-stained haze
when i tear the meat in half!

it's religious! i'm alive!

i have survived every sunday hangover
& treated them all like slumber-party guests.

come visit again!

what i mean is "wasted"
was never the right word for this feeling.

i am full of purpose.

i am making words for every picture in my head.

i'm considering how emdashed i am right now
on this long pause home—how it was never sudden,
or a sharp turn of thought,

just an expansion of my heart
& my mouth about to pop!

& my god i love the world right now
& i love my clothes & all my friends
& i love poems & drunk shimmers
that go on forever
like &&& & never end &

this bit could be a movie, couldn't it—
fade & supercut—

GIRL

(smiling, bent over, throwing up)

I am growing into love!

Against Feeling

If Elon Musk has taught me anything, it's that evolution
  lacks
all feeling. I envy his robots, how I could feed them my
  worst sadness
& they wouldn't grieve, their uncontortioned bodies
  buzzing idly.

I practice detachment with corporate empathy.
When Burger King tweets me, I block their account.
It's easy, deleting my way out of myself

but some days I still pray a Tesla takes me out.
The act is faultless, technological selection,
& I'm grateful for that small steal of a connection,

no matter the hurt. We all want to die touching
beautiful bodies & that's our mistake—
tenderness, the loose screw that breaks us.

our language of accidents

i misspell *angel* & call you
my angle. both are true.

you, my intersection of light beams:

i never know which direction
we gleam, but whenever i speak,
i am speaking towards your shine—

;

my phone capitalizes your whole
name, recognizes love before i do.

my bigtall love growing
beyond my toes!

i'm bringing the whole band

& blasting brass,

shepherding crowds to our porch
to hear my manifesto.

;

autocorrect changes *i love you*
to *i live you.* a supreme truth.

my angle. i live you.

at the end of each night
we find one another
in every mistake we are lucky enough
to own—this backwards network of skies

patched together by texts & throats.

For Crying

Since leaving my mother's womb,
I've breathed out the myth I've made:
how I cried so raw I wrecked windows.

How the doctors gagged me with a striped blanket
& said *this is it, Mary, this is all you get.*
Wouldn't you rather raise a cabbage patch kid?

I wail big, excite loudly, sob out to gods
who guide me, yelling, *yes, this way!*
This way looks the driest!

I can't be shamed into little
emotions. I like my marvelous overflow,
how, each day, I swim through myself.

I don't understand how people can move through life
without wetness in their eyes most times.
It's like they don't even feel beautiful.

When I die, surely there is a crowd of flowers
& a crown of acquaintances who mock
how my body still jerks in its coffin.

Everyone leans forward in awe, fearful
of what I might spit up somehow,
& that's how the truth spills out:

how they always counted my laments
as scandal; how, at my best, I was too alive
for them to handle, my blasphemous body's

inglorious blubbering, this
graced carcass collapsing

                              for good.

Definitions

Some poems in this manuscript are titled after words invented and defined by a random unique Word Generator.

Anaphystopia: *noun.* unpleasant unpleasant surroundings.

Reflekration: *noun.* the action of reflekting the contents of a new bottle.

Seadow: *noun.* a rueful or hurtful state; a painful or bitter one.

Triclops Fusica: *noun.* a deep yellow color; *noun:* a light fog or a layer of small particles in an air or deep sea.

Varnigals: *noun.* the patterns or markings of birds visible in green or yellowish plumage.

Notes

The manuscript title, *Are You There*, refers to the idle Netflix screen, when the viewer's remote has been immobile for so long that the technology reaches out to reawaken them.

The italicized words in "whale poetica" are taken from Madeleine Aggeler's article, "Hundreds of Whales are Dying on Australia's Coast."

"robert kardashian's hologram poetica" takes words from Kim Kardashian's tweet on October 29, 2020.

Some of the italicized words in "schrödinger's poetica" are taken from one of Einstein's letters to Schrödinger.

The italicized words in "transatlanticism poetica" are taken from Death Cab For Cutie's song "Transatlanticism."

"Varnigals" was originally written for a friend.

"A computer falls in love with itself" takes its questions from the article, "Two Artificial Intelligence (AI) Chatbots talk and argue with each other."

"love island poetica" uses words from Jon and Hannah's conversations from season one of Love Island UK.

"dead search engine poetica" refers to the death of the character-based search engine, Jeeves, killed by Ask.com in 2006.

"Diptych" uses a quote from Van Gogh: "The sadness will last forever."

Acknowledgements

To Téa, I live you, my angle. Thank you for always loving me and supporting me.

To my family—Mom, Dad, Madison, Will, Grandma and Grandpa, I love you and am happy to share this with you. Thank you for your support. I never let the dirty bastards get me down.

To Callista, you were the first person who believed in my writing and I'm eternally grateful for that.

To Angela, I would not be here without your support all these years. Thank you for everything.

To James, I did it! Isn't this cool? Thanks for everything.

To Dan Rzicznek, thank you for believing in my thesis and helping me see it through.

To my past friends, I probably miss you, and I have never forgotten your tenderness.

Thank you to all the writers who have supported me along the way, some mentioned previously: Téa Franco, Callista Buchen, Chris Lanyon, Amy Jannotti, Lilia Marie Ellis, Dan Rzicznek, Brandon Noel, Sam Burt, Tony Wade, Freddy LaForce, Shawn Berman, Angelo Maneage, Jarrett Moseley, Adrian Matejka, Raphael Bob-Waksberg, C.T. Salazar and Phil Elverum.

Thank you to Amy Acre and Jake Wild Hall at Bad Betty Press for believing in my work and giving it a wonderful home. I'm so grateful to be a part of it, and I'm always surprised at the care you both have for my poems and personhood.

Thank you to the editors who have held space for my work and have published some of these poems in earlier forms: Brandon and Tony, S. Fey, Isaura Ren, Rachelle Toarmino, Aaron Burch, Kevin Sullivan, Han VanderHart, Chen Chen, Umang Kalra. Thank you to Natalie Solmer, who published my very first poem in 2017 in *The Indianapolis Review*. While it's not a part of this collection, this book wouldn't exist without that first acceptance.

Thank you to my community: my longtime friends; my new friends; my ex-friends; my fellow writers; my professors at Franklin, especially Jennifer Smith, Susan Crisafulli, George Phillips, and Richard Erable; everyone else.

Thank you to my Wellbutrin XL, the Internet, *BoJack Horseman*, my cats, *A Crow Looked at Me*, sunflower fields, the em dash, everyone who has told me to stop watching *BoJack Horseman* because it shows me that you love me even when I don't listen, and everyone and everything that makes me want to keep living.